Through the Storm

Nettie Ann Bowman

Through the Storm

Nettie Ann Bowman

Baptist
Publishing
House

Through the Storm
Baptist Publishing House
ISBN 0-89114-300-9

All scripture quotations contained in this text are from the *Holy Bible, King James Version.*

Printed in the United States of America

Dedication

This book is dedicated to my husband, Ray, whose love has given me the desire to weather the storms; to my entire family who has stood by me during those storms; and to my many WMA friends and fellow church members whose encouragement and help were readily available to me when the storms came.

Acknowledgements

I wish to thank my dear friends Nell Smith and Gail Martin for their many hours of assistance. Without their help this book would not have been possible.

I also express thanks to the national WMA study book committee for asking me to write *Through the Storm.*

Especially do I appreciate Baptist Publishing House for their understanding and patience with me during my most recent illness. To them I say a special thank you.

Contents

Foreword

My mother has been a special gift to me and those fortunate enough to have been touched by her life. She has faced many challenges as a minister's wife, mother, and grandmother. In spite of her serious health problems, her grace, success, and faith have lifted others toward God. Through her life and ministry we have continually witnessed miracles of God's love.

May you find written within these pages the love, joy, comfort, and inspiration needed to help you face your daily obstacles.

I love you, Mother.
Melissa Bowman Speer

This book was written from the heart of a woman who has experienced many trials, tribulations, and heartaches; much of it from physical illnesses. She has endured several major surgeries including four critical heart procedures, and was retained in the hospital for forty days at one time.

With her last surgery she was not expected to live, but faced it with undying faith in her Lord, and encouraged her loved ones and friends to trust Him, never doubting, never wavering. She was an inspiration to all who knew her and many who became acquainted with her.

The strength of this book lies in the author's wisdom of living *through the storms.* As a daughter, pastor's wife, sister, aunt, mother, and grandmother she shares her joys and sorrows.

I have been privileged to be in her home and blessed by her warm spirit of hospitality. I have also had the joy of teaching several ladies retreats where she was the host pastor's wife. Her middle name is organization. No stone was left unturned until everything was just right.

She is a loyal friend, great prayer warrior, and confidante who believes with all her heart that God is the answer no matter what the situation. "What is done for the Lord deserves our best" is her motto.

After reading this book you will find a renewed strength, joy, and faith in facing the storms of your life.

Vi Jensen

Introduction

Tornado, blizzard, hurricane, anger, strife, turmoil — what do these words have in common? They all are storms. Atmospheric or emotional, storms have a profound effect on our lives.

The first three words relate to weather systems that we experience in a physical sense, combinations of which depend on where we live. Meteorologists have sophisticated equipment to track dangerous storms and warn us in advance of the approaching danger. Wisely, we generally seek shelter from nature's tempestuous rage. It is a foolhardy soul that ignores the warnings and continues onward without seeking shelter from the waves of a hurricane or the deadly winds of a killer tornado.

In spite of the warnings, we are sometimes caught in a storm. When the storm hits with all its force, we panic. Like Jesus' disciples in the boat, we wonder how we will survive. How many times have those in peril wished they had taken shelter when the storm warnings were posted?

There are other storm-related elements that we experience in our lives. Depression, loneliness, disappointment, fear, sickness, and death are a few of life's storms that sound the alarm and we ask, "How will we ever survive?" "Why us?" or "Why now?" Where is our shelter when the storm is in full force and the winds of emotional turmoil are ripping the fabric of our fragile lives?

There is comfort, peace, strength, rescue, and protection recorded in God's Word. The Psalmist wrote, *"He maketh the storm a calm, so that the waves thereof are still. Then they are glad because they be quiet; so he bringeth them unto their desired haven"* (Psalm 107:29, 30).

Once when the disciples were in a boat on the

sea, a great storm came. Jesus was asleep in the back of the ship. The disciples were afraid, so they awoke Jesus from his sleep. *"He arose, and rebuked the wind, and said unto the sea, Peace, be still. And the wind ceased, and there was a great calm"* (Mark 4:39). Jesus offered comfort and peace to the disciples as only He could give. *"Blessed be God, even the Father of our Lord Jesus Christ, the Father of mercies, and the God of all comfort; who comforteth us in all our tribulation"* (II Corinthians 1:3, 4).

Have you ever been traveling and a rainstorm came up only to find that your umbrella and raincoat were in the trunk of the car? You were not prepared for the storm.

Are we prepared with our spiritual umbrellas and raincoats when the storms of life assail us? We need God's Word as our rain gear to face the elements of life's storms. Paul advised us to *"Put on the whole armour of God, that ye may be able to stand against the wiles of the devil"* (Ephesians 6:11).

The Psalmist gives this comforting advice: *"God is our refuge and strength, a very present help in trouble. Therefore will not we fear, though the earth be removed, and though the mountains be carried into the midst of the sea; though the waters thereof roar and be troubled, though the mountains shake with the swelling thereof"* (Psalm 46:1-3).

The beautiful old song "Be Still, My Soul" reminds us that God is still in control.

"Be still, my soul: the Lord is on thy side;
Bear patiently the cross of grief or pain;
Leave to thy God to order and provide;
In every change He faithful will remain.
Be still, my soul: thy best, thy heav'nly
  Friend,

Thro' thorny ways leads to a joyful end.

"Be still, my soul: thy God doth undertake
To guide the future as He has the past.
Thy hope, thy confidence let nothing shake;
All now mysterious shall be bright at last.
Be still, my soul: the waves and wind still
know
His voice who ruled them while He dwelt
below."

"The God of Comfort"

I have been through the valley of weeping,
The valley of sorrow and pain;
But the God of all comfort was with me,
At hand to uphold and sustain.

As the earth needs the clouds and the sun-
shine,
Our souls need both sorrow and joy,
So He places us oft in the furnace,
The dross from the gold to destroy.

When He leads through some valley of trouble
His omnipotent hand we can trace
For the trails and sorrows He sends us
As part of His lessons of grace.

Oft we shrink from the purging and pruning,
Forgetting the husbandman knows
That the deeper the cutting and paring
The richer the cluster that grows.

Well He knows that affliction is needed,

He has a wise purpose in view;
And in the dark valley He whispers,
"Hereafter thou shalt know what I do."
As we travel through life's shadowed valley,
Fresh springs of His love ever rise,
And we learn that our sorrow and losses
Are blessings just sent in disguise.

So we'll follow wherever He leads us,
Let the path be dreary or bright,
For we've proved that our God can give comfort,
Or God can give songs in the night."

— Author unknown
From *Heart-Warming Poems*. Sword of the Lord Publishers. Used by permission.

CHAPTER 1

Through the Storms — The Early Years

I was fifteen years old when the first real storm came into my life. My father, Allison Brown, was pastoring his first church, County Line Baptist Church, near Marvell, Arkansas. On a beautiful Sunday afternoon in June, 1953, my sister, Peggy, her husband, Finis Burns, and their two children drove to County Line to attend church with us. After the services they left just ahead of us on the return trip home.

About two or three miles from home we arrived at the scene of a terrible accident. As we approached, we saw that it was Peggy and her family. Their eighteen-month-old daughter, Phyllis, was not seriously hurt, but six-month-old Bert had sustained grave injuries.

We went directly to the hospital praying all the way. Upon our arrival, we found that my sister and her husband had some broken bones and cuts.

Our precious Phyllis was standing by her mother's stretcher crying. She reached up her little arms to me and said, "Aunt Ann." I picked her up, loved her, and gave her to my mother. The doctor was attending to little Bert's head. When the doctor was finished, the nurse gave him to me so I could give him a bottle. He began gasping for breath and died in my arms.

Without the comfort of the Holy Spirit, we could not have faced such a loss. Jesus said, *"Blessed are they that mourn: for they shall be comforted"* (Matthew 5:4). That night in that little room, we felt the peace that only the Comforter can give.

During the time my father ministered at County Line Baptist Church, I met the young man who would become my husband, Ray Bowman. I had always prayed that I would marry a Christian man so our children could be brought up in the nurture and admonition of the Lord. We were married in November, 1954. Our son Stan was born in 1955, and our first daughter, Melissa, was born in 1956.

Melissa was born with allergies to milk and had problems breathing. Her struggle to breathe could be heard throughout the house. The doctor said if she lived to be six months old, she might outgrow the problem.

In April, 1957, Ray and my daddy attended a national associational meeting in Little Rock, Arkansas. Without my knowing about it, Ray surrendered to preach at that meeting. During the afternoon of the same day that Ray surrendered to preach, I noticed that Melissa was breathing normally for the first time in her little life. I believe that if Ray had not answered the call to preach, the Lord would have taken our Melissa from us.

Sometimes God sends severe storms into our lives in order to make us willing to serve Him in the place He wants us to be. Having been a preacher's daughter, I did not really want to be a preacher's wife. However, when God gets our attention, he can also straighten out our *want-to.* Since that day when Melissa's breathing became normal, I have tried to be a blessing to Ray's ministry realizing that God is in charge. I am sure that I have made many mistakes, but if I know my heart, they were not intentional. There have been storms from time to time, but God has stilled the waters every time.

Ray became a pastor in 1957 at Hurricane Baptist Church in the community of Grubbs near Newport, Arkansas. That was a good place to "cut our teeth." We both learned how to love and appreciate God's people. They were such an understanding and caring church. They overlooked our mistakes and loved us anyway.

When Ray accepted that church pastorate, one of the deacons said, "Church, we can make him or break him." When we left, that same deacon said, "Church, I think we've made him."

The three years of that ministry were not always easy. Ray worked full time and we lived fifty miles away. Hurricane had a service on Saturday night instead of Wednesday night so that we could be there. We would travel to the community on Saturday evening and stay until after the evening services on Sunday. We really got to know the people by spending Saturday night with a different family each week.

Ray's next pastorate was the Bradford Baptist Church in Bradford, Arkansas. During our stay there, Ray's mother became very ill and was diagnosed with lupus. She could no longer take care of her mother, who had suffered a stroke and lived with her. So his mother and his grandmother moved in with us. We had two small children, ages four and five, and were expecting a third child.

I experienced some very difficult months as I attempted to manage two small children, a very sick mother-in-law, and a ninety-year-old grandmother. I remember praying for strength and patience each day. I have since learned to take the advice of the popular song, "Lord, teach me today; show me the way to take one day at a time."

Ray's mother died in May, 1960. We were forced to put Grandmother in a nursing home. However, a bright spot came that year; our third child, daughter Karen, was born.

Our ministry at Bradford was very pleasant. We matured in the Lord while living there. Some of the most wonderful people to be found helped us mature. Since I was only twenty-one when Ray accepted that church, I needed a lot of mothering. The older ladies did just that. They helped with the children, taught me how to cook, and made dresses for our girls. I still have a beautiful quilt the ladies in the Women's Missionary Auxiliary made for me. I first became involved in WMA at Bradford. Those ladies were very motivated and were always busy doing something worthwhile. Their enthusiasm was contagious.

While we were at Bradford, the church built its first parsonage. That was the first new house I had ever lived in. We were all so excited about it. I got to show it off every day of the first year we lived there.

The young mothers at Bradford also welcomed me into their lives. Some of us remain very close to this day. When there have been storms in my life, the folks from Bradford are still some of the first to call or come to see me. The Lord allowed us to stay there for five years.

I am comforted as Paul was when he said, *"I thank my God upon every remembrance of you, al-*

ways in every prayer of mine for you all making request with joy, for your fellowship in the gospel from the first day until now; being confident of this very thing, that he which hath begun a good work in you will perform it until the day of Jesus Christ: even as it is meet for me to think this of you all, because I have you in my heart; inasmuch as both in my bonds, and in the defence and confirmation of the gospel, ye all are partakers of my grace. For God is my record, how greatly I long after you all in the bowels of Jesus Christ" (Philippians 1:3-8). I have always found peace in knowing that my Christian friends love me and are praying for me.

In 1962, Ray was in school at Central Baptist College in Conway, Arkansas. One of his instructors, Brother Wallace Glover, said, "Most of our Baptist pastors want to stay right at home. They are not willing to go to the fringe areas where we don't have many churches."

Ray commented that he didn't think he was that way. Brother Glover remarked that he knew a church in Montgomery, Alabama, that had just gone through a storm, yet he felt it had a lot of potential to be a good church. To make a long story short, Ray accepted the pastorate of Rigby Street Baptist Church in July, 1964.

Having never lived outside of Arkansas, I cried for a month when we had to leave Bradford. We had always lived near enough to my parents that we could get to them in a couple of hours. How was I ever going to survive living at least eight or nine hours away? I felt as if I were going to a foreign land. There were very few BMA churches in Alabama at that time, so it was similar to a foreign field of service.

Of all of the churches to which the Lord has allowed us to minister, we probably saw the most growth at Rigby Street. There were some wonderful people there and it was a great place to live. We stayed in Montgomery during most of our children's school years. Those people were really ready for a pastor and had such a sweet spirit.

There were some storms along the way in Alabama, but again God was in control and always calmed the seas when the storms came. The Lord allowed us to stay there for eight years.

From Montgomery, we went to Vardaman Street Baptist Church in Wiggins, Mississippi, which was a wonderful place for a pastor to be. That church really knows how to treat their pastor. Our two oldest children graduated from high school there. Our son, Stan, attended college at Southeastern Baptist College in Laurel, Mississippi. After college, he joined the Navy. One of the worst experiences a mother can have, I suppose, is to see her son join the military. It proved to be a very good experience for him. He retired in 1996, after twenty-two years of service to his country.

While we were at Vardaman Street, Melissa went to Conway, Arkansas, to attend college. She received a full music scholarship for two years at Central Baptist College. While she was standing in line to register, she met her future husband, Ben Speer, who is the youngest of Brother and Mrs. W. R. Speer's children.

In 1975, we left Mississippi to move to Cockrell Hill Baptist Church in Dallas, Texas. The Lord sent us there to teach us patience. I am not sure if we learned that lesson very well. I know we met and loved some of the best people in the world. The Lord allowed us stay there only twenty-two months.

The Lord knew in 1977 that the storms were going to really begin to rage in my life. He was preparing me for what He had in store. He knew where I needed to be to survive those storms.

In September, He sent us back to Bradford. It

was there, during our first stay, that I had experienced all the love and help I needed. God knew how I was going to need those loving and caring people to help me through some really big storms that were heading in my direction. God, in His infinite wisdom, knew just who of His people and where in His kingdom I needed to be. I was going to need the same promise God made to Israel, *"When thou passeth through the waters, I will be with thee;... when thou walkest through the fire, thou shalt not be burned; neither shall the flame kindle upon thee"* (Isaiah 43:2). Then in Isaish 43:5, He said, *"Fear not: for I am with thee."*

Discussion Guide

1. Name one specific storm that you have personally experienced. Share how that storm affected your daily walk with the Lord. Has it been a blessing or a hindrance to your spiritual life?

2. What did you do or what could you have done to make your faith in the Lord stronger?

3. Did you depend upon yourself or the Lord to get you through the storm? Locate a scripture passage that would help you face such a storm with more faith and trust in the Lord. Memorize that scripture.

"When Thou Passest Through the Waters"
Isaiah 43:2

Is there any heart discouraged as it journeys
on its way?
Does there seem to be more darkness than
there is of sunny day?
Oh, it's hard to learn the lesson, as we pass
beneath the rod,
That the sunshine and the shadows serve
alike the will of God!

But there comes a word of promise, like the
promise in the bow —
That, however deep the waters, they shall
never overflow.

When the flesh is worn and weary, and the
spirit is depressed,
And temptations sweep upon it like a storm
on ocean's breast,
There's a haven ever open for the tempest
driven bird,
There's a shelter for the tempted in the prom-
ise of the Word;
For the standard of the Spirit shall be raised
against the foe,
And, however deep the waters, they shall
never overflow.
When a sorrow comes upon you that no other
soul can share,
And the burden seems too heavy for the
human heart to bear;
There is one whose grace can comfort, if you'll
give to Him abode;
For the precious promise reaches to the
depths of human woe,
That, however deep the waters, they shall
never overflow.

When the sands of life are ebbing, and I near
the Jordan's shore,
When I see its waters rising, and I hear its
billows roar,
I will reach my hand to Jesus, in His bosom I
shall hide,
And 'twill only be a moment till I reach the
other side.
It is then the fullest meaning of the promise I
shall know —

"When thou passest through the waters," they
shall never overflow.

Author Unknown
Heart-Warming Poems, Sword of the Lord Publishers. Used by permission.

CHAPTER 2

Through the Storms — The Maturing Years

Ray and I went on our first real vacation in 1978 to visit our son and his family, who lived in Maine. We arrived there on July 4. On July 5, I had a massive heart attack. I had never suspected that I had any heart problems until that day.

To tell you that I lay in that emergency room seventeen hundred miles from home and never asked God *why* would not be the truth. I began to pray and ask God what had I done to bring this trouble. Here I was, just forty years old and trying my best to be actively involved in the Lord's work. I could not understand why this was happening to me.

Sometimes when a young adult dies and leaves a family we say, "It doesn't seem fair." But, God is always fair and does all things well. Still, our carnal natures make us question God. I am so glad that Romans 8:28 is in the Bible. *"We know that all things work together for good to them that love God, to them who are the called according to his purpose."* That verse has brought so much comfort to so many people in times of need.

My two-week stay in the hospital in Brunswick, Maine, was traumatic, a real learning experience for me. There I told the Lord, "I don't understand, but if you can get any glory out of this, I give myself to you." I was able to leave the hospital and fly home.

I am really looking forward to going home to heaven. My homecoming to Bradford after that ordeal in Maine was wonderful; but it was nothing to compare with the homecoming I'll enjoy when I get to heaven. I think of the words of a song, "What a day that will be;/When my Jesus I shall see./ What a day, glorious day, that will be."

After I returned to Bradford, I made an appointment with a cardiologist in Searcy, Arkansas. He put me on medication and said I should be as good as new in a few weeks. However, that did not happen and in December, 1978, I had my first open-heart surgery.

The surgeon came out and told my family that he was only able to do one bypass, which was really all he had expected after seeing the film of my heart. He also said, "If things go well, she should live about two years."

Medically speaking, that may have been true, but when the Lord is in control, things are different. I do not understand, but I do not ask why. God has allowed me to live with this severe heart problem for twenty years. I have tried to keep a positive attitude. Sometimes, I allow the old devil to talk to me and make me feel sorry for myself.

Since 1978, I have been on massive doses of heart medication that cost about three to four hundred dollars a month. The Lord has used His people to help with this need. On one occasion I needed three hundred dollars worth of medicine, and would you believe it, when the mail came that day, there was a check for three hundred and fifty dollars to use wherever we needed it. The Lord has used many people to take care of our needs all through the years. We have experienced the true meaning of *"My God shall supply all your need according to his riches in glory by Christ Jesus"* (Philippians 4:19).

In 1979, my dad passed away at the age of sixty-nine with congestive heart failure. That was a storm that was hard for me to weather. Dad and I had always been very close. Dad was a man of few words, but he always had the right words to calm my fears. When I faced a storm and didn't know which way to turn, he would say, "Nettie Ann, it's going to be all right."

God never puts more on us than he puts in us. He supplies the strength we need to bear our burdens. How true I have found that to be. God's strength is always available when we have come to the end of our own. I remember the words of Isaiah, *"Behold, God is my salvation; I will trust, and not be afraid: for the LORD JEHOVAH is my strength and my song; he also is become my salvation"* (Isaiah 12:2).

The twenty-seventh Psalm has become a special blessing to my life. Notice some of the promises in these verses. *"The LORD is my light and my salvation; whom shall I fear? the LORD is the strength of my life; of whom shall I be afraid? I had fainted, unless I had believed to see the goodness of the LORD in the land of the living. Wait on the LORD: be of good courage, and he shall strengthen thine heart: wait, I say, on the LORD"* (Psalm 27:1, 13, 14). Without the strength of the Lord, the storms of life would overwhelm us.

Our second grandson was born in 1981 with health problems. He had a collapsed lung and was in and out of the hospital repeatedly the first year of his life. When a baby is sick, adults feel so helpless. It is so comforting to know that you can pray and God is right there with you. Once again, the Lord answered our prayers and today, our grandson is a fine young man.

His mother's faith was much stronger than mine during that time of illness. She was such a blessing and strength to me as we sat in that intensive care waiting room. She always knew that he was going to be all right. She assured me that God was hearing our prayers and was going to answer in His own way and in His own time. Meanwhile, we just had to wait. Again the words of the Psalmist were comforting, *"Wait on the LORD: be of good courage, and he shall strengthen thine heart: wait, I say, on the LORD."* Isn't it wonderful when we can wait and watch God at work in our own lives and in the lives of others? God's ways are higher than our ways. *"For as the heavens are higher than the earth, so are my ways higher than your ways, and my thoughts than your thoughts"* (Isaiah 55:9).

Our son was in a terrible car accident in 1981. When I first saw him, I thought he would never look normal again. His head was swollen to twice its regular size. I remember begging God to let him live. Stan was a very good singer. At that time he was not really using his talent for the Lord. I prayed that the Lord would cause him to see that his life had been spared to be a blessing for the cause of Christ. He is now our music director at Bodcaw Baptist Church.

One of the blackest storms I ever encountered came in 1982 when Stan went through a divorce. Watching your children and grandchildren hurt makes a mother's heart break. Stan had a little six-year-old girl. Because Stan was away in the Navy we got to keep her every other weekend. We had some quality time to bond with her. I have prayed every day for her all of her life. She is happily married today and has a precious little girl of her own, our great-grandchild.

One of my friends had gone through her daughter's divorce a few years earlier and did not handle it very well at all. We talked and prayed together about it many times. I remember thinking then, *If this ever happens to one of my children, I will handle it better.* Well, it did happen and I didn't cope very well either. I believe God allows us to face these kinds of storms so we can empathize with others and minister to them. In this way, God can use us to be a blessing to others.

It is difficult to prevent bitterness when your children are going through trials such as divorce. The devil can use those circumstances to create a bitter attitude. Bitterness is not easily overcome, so we must use caution to keep it from rearing its ugly head. God's Word cautions us not to become bitter. *"Looking diligently lest any man fail of the grace of God; lest any root of bitterness springing up trouble you, and thereby many be defiled"* (Hebrews 12:15). Paul also reminded us, *"Let all bitterness ... be put away from you"* (Ephesians 4:31).

I found that in order to keep bitterness from troubling me, I had to pray earnestly for it to be removed and pray for the persons involved. I had to invest a lot of time praying until I had cleared my thoughts of all ill toward those who had hurt my family. I knew I could not effectively serve the Lord nor my family without clearing my life of all ill feelings. I stayed on my knees praying until the burden lifted and I could think of the situation and people without my emotions giving way to bad thoughts.

I began to have fainting spells in June, 1983. We were living in Blytheville, Arkansas, where Ray was pastor of Fairview Baptist Church. My doctor there sent me to Memphis for tests. After the results were back, I was told that I could not leave the hospital without open-heart surgery. After my first surgery, I said I would never have that again; but you never really know what you will do when you have no choice. My choices were surgery or death. If it had not been for my family the choice would have been easy. My family gathered around my bed and asked me to go through the surgery for them. We prayed together and I agreed to do it for them. I had my second open-heart surgery that month. I felt somewhat better after the surgery, but had to remain on massive doses of heart medication.

In 1984, our daughter Karen was expecting a baby. Her doctor suspected there might be problems. She called me to go with her for some tests. The doctor told us it looked like the baby's head was two months ahead of its body in development.

The drive back to Karen's house was filled with tears. Why should this happen to us? We were crying and praying. Karen couldn't understand it all; yet she was a nurse and knew enough to be concerned. I said to her, "Karen, God must have thought you are a very special person to give you a child like that; if it is to be."

Karen didn't say anything for a while. Then she said, "Maybe so; I know I wouldn't love it any less. I would give it lots of tender love and care." She smiled and said, "If that's what the Lord has for me, I can handle it." Another of my daughters had proved to me that God's grace is sufficient.

When Paul went to the Lord requesting that his thorn in the flesh be removed, he received an answer, *"My grace is sufficient for thee: for my strength is made perfect in weakness."* Paul responded, *"Most gladly therefore, will I rather glory in my infirmities, that the power of Christ may rest upon me"* (II Corinthians 12:9).

Karen returned for more tests two months later and everything was fine. Sometimes God has to let us know He is in control and allow us to depend upon Him when things are out of our control. Then, and then only, are we able to say, "If that is your will, Lord; with your grace, it is going to be fine with me." Sure enough, two days before Mother's Day in 1984, Karen received the greatest gift possible, a healthy baby boy.

Many times we have to learn to just let go of self and let God have His way in our lives. "Letting go and letting God" brings to mind the picture of a child standing on the side of a swimming pool or lake, hesitant to jump into the arms of the waiting parent. The parent offers encouragement and promises support if the child will just trust and jump in. The child considers all the possibilities and finally relinquishes his fears and leaps into the water, proving his trust, and is borne up by a loving parent.

Letting go of our fears and just trusting God to bear us up is the key to getting through the worst storms life can bring. Believing in our hearts that He is in control and knows all things assures us that we are safe. How often we fret and struggle against the storms of life, worrying over every possibility, forgetting that God is there to bear us up. We allow fear to close our spiritual ears to the encouragement He offers. We pace back and forth, thinking about how deep and dark the water is instead of focusing on the wonderful, loving parent waiting for us to trust.

I once attended a Sunday School class with a severely handicapped girl and her mother. I thought about how we take for granted one of God's great miracles — the health and welfare of our children. Many times since then I have thanked God for being so good to us to give us three children, six grandchildren, and one great-grandchild who are all perfectly healthy. I am so ungrateful many times for the things God has blessed me with. I need to practice what Paul commanded, *"In every thing give thanks: for this is the will of God in Christ Jesus concerning you"* (I Thessalonians 5:18). It is hard to thank and praise God during the storm, but it is possible.

Back in the sixties, Ray and I went with my dad to a national association meeting in Gatlinburg, Tennessee. As we were admiring the mountains, Daddy said, "Anyone who can see this and doubt there is a God has to be out of his mind."

I remember saying, "Yes, but look at those valleys. Without them, the mountains would not be nearly so beautiful." I believe we are made more beautiful by the valleys — or storms — God allows to come into our lives.

Knowing He is our strength, when we walk in stormy places, we need not fear. We can radiate joy and gladness in the midst of the shadows. As the diamond shows greater brilliance with more cuts, so our lives shine brighter with greater polish through the many storms the heavenly Father allows to come our way. Hardships and sorrow can bring forth confidence and strength. One way we can face these storms is to know, as the song "God on the Mountain" tells us, the God of the good times is still God in the bad times.

"God on the Mountain"
by Tracy G. Dartt

Life is easy when you're up on the mountain

And you've got peace of mind
Like you've never known,
But when things change
And you're down in the valley,
Don't lose faith for you're never alone.
The God on the mountain is still God in the valley,
When things go wrong,
He'll make them right.
And the God of the good times is still God in the bad times,
The God of the day is still God of the night.
We talk of faith when we're up on the mountain,
But talk comes easy
When life's at its best,
But in the valley of trials and temptations,
That's when faith is put to test."

In December, 1985, the Lord led us to Landmark Baptist Church in England, Arkansas. We had many large medical bills while there and without the financial assistance of God's people at Landmark, we would have suffered much hardship. They provided for our needs and the Lord used them to be a very special blessing to us.

Another big storm invaded our lives in 1985. My mother had lived alone since Dad died and had done really well. However, we began to notice that she wasn't the same. She began to forget things more frequently. She talked and acted differently. We took her to Memphis to a doctor who ordered an MRI. The results indicated Alzheimers Disease. He said we needed to begin to look for a place where she could be cared for. My sisters and I all dreaded the day we would have to tell Mother.

One day Ray and I were visiting with her. She would hardly ever spend the night with any of us. As I get older I understand that feeling. That day, when I asked her to come home with us, she said, "Net, I believe I will." She told me that being alone made her afraid of everything and she could not sleep well. I told her she could stay with Ray and me, but she said, "No, Net, there is a new retirement home in Forrest City. I want to move in there."

I thought *Thank you, Lord.* I called my sisters and we met with Mother at the home. She didn't want to go home; so we got what she needed and settled her in her new home. As my Aunt Doris would say, "God was in the plan all the time."

In 1990, we moved to the First Baptist Church in Mantachie, Mississippi. We continued to care for and visit Mother in Forrest City. Those were four hard years. Watching a beautiful, gracious, neat, caring lady being reduced to a mere vegetable was almost more than we could bear. There are some things worse than death. Mother died in 1991 and we could actually praise God for calling her home to a place prepared just for her where she was alive and alert.

Discussion Guide

1. Has your family faced difficult storms? How did you cope? Did you depend on the Lord? What did you or could you have done to show your family you depended on the Lord?

2. Has ill health caused a storm in your family? How have you found comfort in the Lord? Share scripture, songs, or poetry that gives you strength to face another day.

3. Has bitterness crept into your heart? What does the Bible say about bitterness? What steps can you take to overcome that bitterness?

4. Has your family faced dealing with the ill health of parents? Share how the Lord guided you through it. How can you help someone else going through a similar situation? If you found comfort in books or scripture, share those with the group.

5. Has a friend had serious storms in life? Were you able to help? What can you do to help friends who are going through storms?

Note: Sometimes God brings storms in one's life because of sin. He intends to teach the person through the storms. Be sure you do not interfere with God's plans. Any assistance you offer should be done in love and under God's direction. You may even need to consult your pastor in private before offering to help a friend or another church member. He may know things you don't know and may not be free to share them. Respect that privacy.

"How the Lord Sustains"
"Cast thy burden upon the LORD, and he shall sustain thee" (Psalm 55:22).

Christian, when thy way seems darkest,
When thine eyes with tears are dim,
Straight to God thy Father hast'ning,
Tell thy troubles all to Him.
Not to human ear confiding
Thy sad tale of grief and care,
But before thy Father kneeling,
Pour out all thy sorrows there.

Sympathy of friends may cheer thee
When the fierce, wild storms have burst,
But God only can console thee
When it breaks upon thee first.
Go with words, or tears, or silence,
Only lay thee at His feet;
Thou shalt prove how great His pity,

And His tenderness how sweet.

Think, too, thy divine Redeemer
Knew as thou canst never know
All the deepest depths of suffering,
All the weight of human woe;
And though now in glory seated
He can hear thy feeblest cry,
Even hear the stifled sighing
Of thy dumb heart's agony.
All thy griefs by Him are ordered;
Needful is each one for thee;
Every tear by Him is counted,
One too much there cannot be.
And if, whilst they fall so thickly,
Thou canst own His way is right,
Then each bitter tear of anguish
Precious is in Jesus' sight.

Far too well thy Saviour loves thee
To allow thy life to be
One long, calm, unbroken summer,
One unruffled, stormless sea.
He would have thee fondly nestling
Closer to His loving breast;
He would have that world seem brighter,
Where alone is perfect rest.

Though His wise and loving purpose
Clearly yet thou mayest not see,
Still believe with faith unshaken,
All will work for good to thee.
Therefore, when thy way is gloomy,
And thine eyes with tears are dim,
Straight to God thy Father hast'ning,
Tell thy sorrows all to Him.

Author Unknown
From *Heart-Warming Poems,* Sword of the Lord Publishers. Used by permission.

CHAPTER 3

Weathering the Storms

Our years at Mantachie were full of storms, but we were just where the Lord wanted us as we weathered some very trying times. The people there provided for our needs and even a lot of our wants. They were very gracious and caring people.

In 1993, I began to suffer shortness of breath and chest pains. The pain became so severe I could not do anything at all. I could not even get out of bed. While in the hospital, the doctor told me that it was impossible to leave the hospital without surgery. My heart was a time-bomb, ready to explode.

In June I had my third open-heart surgery. The procedure required going through my back, which is called thoracic heart surgery. That was by far the worst surgery of any I had endured. That night after the surgery the hospital staff had to call a Code Blue on me. That code meant my heart had actually stopped. Because I was bleeding internally, I was given eight pints of blood. The doctor never really explained it all, but he said they had almost lost me. In the process of the surgery a nerve was severed in my back. The pain became unbearable. I had to go to a pain doctor in Memphis for shots to block the nerve for a year after the surgery. It still bothers me a lot even today.

In the summer of 1994, unknown to us, our daughter Karen was experiencing a storm of her own. Her marriage of fourteen years fell apart. Again we were facing the storm of divorce in our family. I asked the Lord why was this happening to us again. Those were dark days, especially for our ten-year-old grandson. Karen had tried to distance herself from us so we would not worry. Not knowing is sometimes worse than knowing.

I tried to assure her of our love for her. We were there to help her when she needed us. We discovered again that when a child hurts, so does her mother. Karen's divorce was finalized in August, 1995. Today, she is a happy, single mom. She and her son now live near us, which is a blessing to both them and us. Having our grandson nearby means I can give him a lot of tender loving care. He is now a teenager, is an honor student, and is a well-adjusted, wonderful Christian young man who is a leader in the youth group at our church.

Through all these storms of life, God has been communicating with me. He has never left my side. He has comforted me and my family with His Word. He has guided us safely.

God communicates with us through His Word, through prayer, and through suffering. In the last twenty years I know I have experienced all three. Without the first two, I could not have endured the last one.

The Twenty-Third Psalm has been, and is still

today, a place to find peace and comfort. I have learned a lot about my shepherd while studying these verses. As you read the psalm, notice the benefits that come as a result of the Shepherd's care.

"The LORD is my shepherd; I shall not want. He maketh me to lie down in green pastures: he leadeth me beside the still waters. He restoreth my soul: he leadeth me in the paths of righteousness for his name's sake. Yea, though I walk through the valley of the shadow of death, I will fear no evil: for thou art with me; thy rod and thy staff they comfort me. Thou preparest a table before me in the presence of mine enemies: thou anointest my head with oil; my cup runneth over. Surely goodness and mercy shall follow me all the days of my life: and I will dwell in the house of the LORD for ever."

If we are going to experience the Shepherd's care, we must first realize that we need the shepherd. As sheep need a shepherd to survive, so do we.

Sheep are not smart animals. Without a shepherd, they would go the wrong way, not aware of the dangers ahead. It is said that sheep have been known to eat their way right off the mountainside. They will eat and drink things that are bad for them. Sheep can get down, not be able to get up, and will, without assistance, eventually die.

God reveals the blessing of our having a shepherd. *"Now the God of peace, that brought again from the dead our Lord Jesus, that great shepherd of the sheep, through the blood of the everlasting covenant, make you perfect in every good work to do his will, working in you that which is wellpleasing in his sight, through Jesus Christ; to whom be glory for ever and ever. Amen"* (Hebrews 13:20, 21). We, the little sheep, need to take a good look at ourselves and realize we cannot make it in this dangerous world without our Shepherd. Believing in our Shepherd, we will know a life of perfect rest and contentment, no matter what our circumstances.

It is so important that we know our Shepherd. There is no want if we are His sheep. Psalm 22 shows us the Good Shepherd who lays down His life for the sheep. Psalm 23 shows Him as our Great Shepherd, providing our needs. Psalm 24 shows us our Chief Shepherd who is to come again. Before the Lord can function as our Great Shepherd, we must first know Him as our Good Shepherd. John tells us, *"Then said Jesus unto them again, Verily, verily, I say unto you, I am the door of the sheep"* (John 10:7). There is no other way to become God's sheep except by Jesus. Jesus further states, *"All that ever came before me are thieves and robbers: but the sheep did not hear them. I am the door: by me if any man enter in, he shall be saved, and shall go in and out, and find pasture. The thief cometh not, but for to steal, and to kill, and to destroy: I am come that they might have life, and that they might have it more abundantly"* (John 10:8-10).

In your storms of life, are you secure enough to say with confidence, *"The LORD is my shepherd; I shall not want."*?

Have you ever felt caught in a situation that seemed absolutely unbearable? You begin to think, *this couldn't be happening to me*. You wonder how you will survive, or if you will survive.

The little sheep in the pasture panic with just a clap of thunder. They wonder where the shepherd is. The true shepherd is always nearby, ready to protect and guide the sheep to safety.

We can know, as the Shepherd's little sheep, He is watching over us. *"He shall feed his flock like a shepherd: he shall gather the lambs with his arm, and carry them in his bosom, and shall gently lead those that are with young*" (Isaiah 40:11). Beloved sheep, everything that happens in our lives is noticed by our Shepherd. We can know that He will accomplish His purpose in our lives because we are His sheep. Our Shepherd never leaves us. He will complete that which He has begun in us to conform us to His image. All that God begins, He completes. He is the God of finished work.

So, rest, little sheep, your Shepherd is nearby. He is in control. Remember, whatever comes into our lives has passed by Him and it will accomplish God's purpose for us. He does all things well.

I feel sure that without the promises in Psalm 23, I could not have faced the storm of 1993. Without my Good Shepherd and God's wonderful people, the storm would have been a lot darker. I could think of the fact that God had brought me this far and look at all the things God's people were doing that were blessings to me life. I could always see a beautiful rainbow on the horizon.

Throughout the year of 1994, I made progress and the Lord saw fit for us to move to a smaller church. It seems like He handpicked Bodcaw Baptist Church in Bodcaw, Arkansas, for us at this stage of our lives. My dad had been pastor of this church back in the sixties. I recognized a few of the names and faces. Dad had told me that Bodcaw was one of the best churches he had ever pastored. I can relate to that now.

About two weeks after we moved to Bodcaw in 1995, our son, Stan, had a heart attack. We were seventeen hundred miles from him and I was not physically able to make the trip to Maine. Ray was afraid to leave me alone, so our daughter flew up there to be with Stan. They kept us informed of his progress. Those were some dark, stormy days until we found out he was going to be all right. Again, I felt the comfort of my Shepherd.

In May of that same year, I had to have gall bladder surgery. Because of my heart condition, I had to go to Memphis for the surgery. I felt the prayers of God's people and the presence of God's Holy Spirit as I entered that surgery. Everything went smoothly throughout the surgery. I thought, *well, surely, this is the last storm for a while.* For two years, it was.

Of all the storms I have told you about, the next one hurt the most. Our oldest grandson entered college. He had been reared in a strict Christian home with wonderful and loving parents. He chose to go to a secular college. He got involved with *friends* who were not Christians and he began to live a worldly life. God got his attention in a vivid way and he had to pay dearly for his wandering. He does not fault the others for his foolish decisions, but takes full responsibility himself.

Every time I talked to him during his ordeal, I tried to encourage him in the Lord. He would assure me that he knew he was saved. I prayed more and shed more tears over him than in any of the other storms. I prayed that God would put his loving arms around him and shield him from death or trouble. The few months were long, but we all grew in the Lord throughout this ordeal. When there is nothing you can do but pray, you do a lot of praying. I prayed myself to sleep a lot of nights.

Our grandson is now back in college near us and doing well in life. He seems to be close to the Lord. He has met a fine Christian girl with whom he feels he can spend the rest of his life. I know that if he doesn't stay close to the Lord, he is open prey for Satan. I continue to pray that he will stay close to the Lord and serve Him only.

In February, 1997, I kept an appointment with my cardiologist. He put me in the hospital for a few tests. The results were not good. I only had one artery feeding enough blood to my heart. The doctor said, "Your heart is in very bad condition with scar tissue; those bad arteries are not good enough to hold a graft." I continued to be on massive doses of heart medication. If there is one thing I have learned from all these storms, it is this: I have been sheltered in the arms of God through it all.

My mind goes back to the time Ray and I took our daughter, Melissa, to college in Conway, Arkansas. We lived in Mississippi at that time, so to avoid such a long trip in one day, we stayed overnight at a motel on the way. Our plans were to leave Little Rock at 4:00 a.m. to return to our home in Mississippi. Our gas gauge registered empty. We drove about ten miles and did not find a gas station that was open, so we decided to wait at one until it opened. We had about a thirty-minute wait. You can imagine the complaining we did because we had gotten up as planned and here we were in the car waiting when we could have been in the motel still sleeping.

Finally, the station opened; we got our gas and went on our way. About an hour down the road, there had been a terrible accident. Had we not been detained, we probably would have been there about the time it happened. We suddenly realized our Shepherd had been watching over us all the time.

Oh, little sheep, why do we get so upset? Are our steps not ordered by the Shepherd? *"The steps of a good man are ordered by the LORD: and he delighteth in his way"* (Psalm 37:23). We need to walk by faith and know that goodness and mercy are following us all the days of our lives because the Lord is our Shepherd. We need to be calm and know that we are to rest and give thanks in everything for it is in the will of God.

If God makes us wait, He sees it not as loss, but

gain. This may not be the way we had planned, but our times are in the hands of a sovereign God; therefore, dear sheep, we need to rest. We worry, fret, and complain even though Psalm 23:2 tells us, *"He maketh me to lie down in green pastures: he leadeth me beside the still waters."*

According to Phillips Keller's book, *A Shepherd Looks at Psalm 23*, sheep must be free of four things before they can rest. First, they must be free from hunger if they are to rest. We learn in Psalm 23:2 that our hunger needs have been met. The Shepherd has seen to that. Just as the sheep will not lie down if they are hungry, neither will Christians find rest if they do not feed on God's Word. As the Shepherd says, *"The words that I speak unto you, they are spirit, and they are life"* (John 6:63). *"Man shall not live by bread alone, but by every word that proceedeth out of the mouth of God"* (Matthew 4:4). Dear ones, are you wandering about, unable to rest, searching for something, getting all messed up because you won't spend time feeding in the pastures the Shepherd has prepared for you? Get into His Word and feed your spirit and soul.

Second, if sheep are to rest, they must be free from fear. If large animals attack, they are so helpless without the care of their Shepherd. Are we so filled with fears that we cannot rest in Jesus? Sheep run when they are afraid. A sudden noise can cause panic in the sheepfold. The sheep run in every direction when fear strikes. Running is the only cure as far as the sheep are concerned. Have you, as a child of God, ever wanted to run when you were overcome with fear? The shepherd of the sheep is aware of their fear immediately and moves to reassure them of his presence. They are no longer afraid when they realize the shepherd is near and protecting them. The same should be true for those who are God's children. *"The LORD is my shepherd; I shall not want."* He allows us to lie down in green pastures and rest. We need not panic.

Fear is not of God. Paul advised Timothy that *"God hath not given us the spirit of fear; but of power, and of love, and of a sound mind"* (II Timothy 1:7). We need to remember that anything that happens to us must be filtered through God's sovereign fingers of love.

Third, the sheep must be free of friction. Sheep fear they may be attacked by other sheep and feel they must defend themselves. Have we not had times in our lives when we felt we needed to defend ourselves when we really needed to just let our Shepherd defend us?

Fourth, sheep cannot rest unless they are free from pests. Like sheep, we can be distracted by ugly, ungodly people that keep us in a turmoil. We need to recognize that our Shepherd will help us keep our lives free from these pests.

Are some of these things holding us prisoner keeping us from sleep and rest? We need to give these things to our Shepherd so we can rest.

The wages of sin do so weigh us down! Why do we allow this to happen when we have a good Shepherd who wishes to free us from that weight? Is it because we do not know the Shepherd or have we refused to follow Him?

"All we like sheep have gone astray; we have turned every one to his own way" (Isaiah 53:6). *"Before I was afflicted I went astray"* (Psalm 119:67). Sometimes when a sheep is stubborn and will not stay with the flock, but is always trying to go his own way, the shepherd has to break its leg. That may sound severe, but the sheep cannot wander with a broken leg. The shepherd's purpose is not to cripple the sheep, but to teach a

valuable lesson. The shepherd then binds the sheep's leg and holds him to his bosom. He lovingly carries the sheep until the broken bone is healed. Brokenness has brought it to the bosom of the shepherd. When the leg is mended, the sheep, having grown accustomed to a close relationship with the shepherd, will follow at his side. *"The sacrifices of God are a broken spirit: a broken and a contrite heart, O God, thou wilt not despise"* (Psalm 51:17).

Friends, have we not been prone to wander from the fold of God? Sometimes storms must be allowed by God in our lives so that we might get back into a close relationship with our Shepherd. Let's not allow these storms to make us bitter, but better.

In verse four of Psalm 23, we find that sometimes the path the Shepherd has chosen for us is in a dark valley. I have found that it is in a valley that the Shepherd has revealed himself to me as the Good Shepherd. Valleys are designed to show us that we don't need to fear, for the Lord, our Shepherd, is with us.

The staff of the shepherd is a picture of the Holy Spirit. The shepherd, many times guides his sheep with his staff. It serves as an extra hand to get the sheep where they need to be or out of something they don't need to be in. The staff identifies the Shepherd.

Isn't it wonderful to know that the Holy Spirit is our comforter? *"Hope maketh not ashamed; because the love of God is shed abroad in our hearts by the Holy Ghost which is given unto us"* (Romans 5:5). This verse, as well as Romans 8:1-9, helps us to become more familiar with the ministry of the Holy Spirit. Take time to make a study of these verses. The Holy Spirit is truly our Comforter.

One of the main reasons that some Christians

seem to have a more intimate relationship with the heavenly Father is that they have come to know the purpose, and thus, the comfort of their Shepherd's rod. The rod is an extension of the shepherd's arm. The Shepherd's rod, like God's Word, is a weapon of power, of protection, and defense. The shepherd uses his rod to guide the sheep to the green pastures, to lift his sheep from danger, and to protect the sheep from intruders into the sheepfold. Truly the shepherd and his rod are comfort to the sheep.

Discussion Guide

1. Review the responsibility the shepherd has for the sheep. How are Christians like sheep?
2. Write Psalm 23 on a card or purchase it in some form and place it in your home in a place where your family members can be reminded of the shepherd's care.
3. Memorize Psalm 23.

"My Grace Is Sufficient for Thee"

When sin-stained, burdened and weary,
From bondage I longed to be free,
Then came to my heart a sweet message,
"My grace is sufficient for thee."

Though tempted and sadly discouraged,
My soul to this refuge will flee,
And rest in the blessed assurance;
"My grace is sufficient for thee."

My bark may be tossed by the tempest
That sweeps o'er the turbulent sea —
A rainbow illumines the darkness:
"My grace is sufficient for thee."
O Lord, I would press on with courage

Though rugged the pathway may be,
Sustained and upheld by the promise:
"My grace is sufficient for thee."

Soon, soon the warfare will be over,
My Lord face to face I shall see,
And prove, as I dwell in His presence,
"My grace is sufficient for thee."

Author Unknown
From *Heart-Warming Poems.* Sword of the Lord Publishers. Used by permission.

CHAPTER 4

Through the Storms: Count It All Joy

The book of Philippians is a joyful letter written to Christians. Christians have the privilege of experiencing joy. The Psalmist said, *"Thou wilt shew me the path of life: in thy presence is fulness of joy; at thy right hand there are pleasures for evermore"* (Psalm 16:11). What happens to our joy? We allow many circumstances to steal our joy.

Paul had every reason, from our point of view, not to be joyful. He was a prisoner in Rome. Epaphroditus was sent by the church in Philippi to bring an offering and comfort to Paul. In the midst of prison, Paul wrote the church a joyful letter of thanks. *"I sent him therefore the more carefully, that, when ye see him again, ye may rejoice, and that I may be the less sorrowful. Receive him therefore in the Lord with all gladness; and hold such in reputation: because for the work of Christ he was nigh unto death, not regarding his life, to supply your lack of service toward me"* (Philippians 2:25-30).

Paul wanted to go to Rome to preach the gospel; instead he was there as a prisoner. The believers were divided. Some were for Paul and some against him. Paul's decision was already made. He wasn't going to let his circumstances rob him of his joy. Perhaps one reason Christians do not influence more people for Christ is that, in the midst of the storm, we do not act like God is in control.

A thorough study of Philippians ought to convince us that we can live a life of Christian joy in spite of circumstances, people, or things. We don't need to worry when circumstances get difficult or when the storm clouds of life rage. Some people seem to thrive on worry and are proud of it in spite of what Jesus said, *"Therefore take no thought, saying, What shall we eat? or, What shall we drink? or, Wherewithal shall we be clothed? (For after these things do the Gentiles seek:) for your heavenly Father knoweth that ye have need of all these things. But seek ye first the kingdom of God, and his righteousness; and all these things shall be added unto you. Take therefore no thought for the morrow: for the morrow shall take thought for the things of itself. Sufficient unto the day is the evil thereof"* (Matthew 6:31-34).

When we find ourselves losing our joy, we need to ask ourselves some questions: Are we groping for things? Are we double-minded? Are we proud? Are we worrying? If the answer is yes, then it is time to ask God to cleanse us from our sin, forgive us, and restore our minds and hearts as they ought to be. We can know joy that defeats worry and fills us with the peace of God. For further references, study the fourth chapter of Philippians. Verses 1-9 show us God's peace; verses 10-13 show us God's power, and verses 14-23 show us God's provision. What more can we ask from God than peace, power, and provision?

The single mind that Paul refers to so much in Philippians simply means it makes no difference what happens to me, just as long as Christ is glorified and the gospel is shared with others. We should count it all joy when God chooses us to go through the storms that God might be glorified through us.

As I mentioned previously, Paul wanted to go to Rome to preach, but God chose to send him in chains to spend his time at Rome in prison. The same God that used Moses' rod, Gideon's pitcher, and David's sling, used Paul's chains. As he wrote later while in prison. *"I suffer trouble, as an evil doer, even unto bonds; but the word of God is not bound"* (II Timothy 2:9). He did not complain about his chains. He was able to witness to the lost. He was chained to a Roman soldier. I am sure that being chained to a man who prayed without ceasing caused some of them to put their trust in Christ. Sometimes God has to put chains on His people to accomplish something that we may otherwise never accomplish.

My prayer is that in some way I have been a blessing to someone through the stormy chains God has allowed to come my way. Because of Paul's chains, Christ was known by many. *"My bonds in Christ are manifest in all the palace, and in all other places "* (Philippians 1:13). Because of Paul's critics, Christ was preached. He said, *"What then? notwithstanding, every way, whether in pretence, or in truth, Christ is preached; and I therein do rejoice, yea, and will rejoice"* (Philippians 1:18). Christ was magnified because of Paul's ministry while in prison. *"According to my earnest expectation and my hope, that in nothing I shall be ashamed, but that with all boldness, as always, so now also Christ shall be magnified in my body, whether it be by life, or by death"* (Philippians 1:20). That is also our reason for living — to magnify Christ. As the unsaved watch a saved person go through a storm, they can see Jesus magnified.

Paul said, *"For to me to live is Christ, and to die is gain"* (Philippians 1:21). Paul was convinced that Christ would have him remain to further the gospel and to further their joy and faith.

We need to ask ourselves often, "Am I conducting myself in a manner worthy of the gospel?" We should walk worthy of the calling we have in Christ. (See Ephesians 4:1) People are watching us. Do they see Christ is our lives?

You are writing a gospel,
A chapter each day,
By the deed that you say.
Men read what you write,
Whether faithful or true:
Just what is the gospel
According to you?"

From *The Sword of the Lord.* Used by permission.

Discussion Guide

1. Has a storm in your life brought joy to you and your family? Name an instance or situation when you thought a situation appeared destructive, but soon realized that God meant it for good. Share with the group how you found joy.

2. Choose a verse in Philippians that brings comfort or challenge to you. Write it on a card and place it where it will remind you of God's care for you and your family. Memorize that verse.

3. Does your church have a benevolent heart? Does it or your ladies group have a benevolence

committee? If so, how does that committee function to bring comfort and joy to those who are hurting?

4. What could your church do to show more love to the hurting in your church and community?

5. What can you do to create more love and a benevolent spirit in your church family? Name some specific ways women can show a benevolent spirit.

6. Make specific plans for a benevolent project and carry out those plans.

7. Has your church weathered storms that affected the spiritual growth of the church? Is there remaining bitterness?

8. What specific steps can you or your group take to bring about healing of bitterness. Sometimes all you can do is to pray. Beware of gossip. Pray for the bitterness to be removed. Show love one to another in all your actions, deeds, and words.

"Does He Care?"

What can it mean? Is it aught to Him
That the days are long, and the nights are
 dim?
Can He be touched by the griefs I bear,
Which sadden the heart and whiten the hair?
About His throne are eternal calms,
And strong glad music of happy psalms,
And bliss unruffled by any strife —
How can He care for my little life?

And yet, I want Him to care for me,
While I live in this world where sorrows be.
When the lights die down from the path I
 take;

When strength is feeble and friends forsake;
And love and music which once did bless,
Have left me to silence and loneliness;
Then my life-song changes to sobbing prayers,
And my heart cries out for a God who cares.

When shadows hand o'er the whole day long,
And my sprit is bowed with shame and wrong,
And I am not good, and the bitter shade
Of conscious sin makes my soul afraid;
And the busy world has too much to do
To stay in its courses to help me through;
And I long for a Saviour — can it be
That the God of the universe cares for me?
Oh, wonderful story of deathless Love,
Each child is dear to that heart above!
He fights for me when I cannot fight;
He comforts me in the gloom of night;
He lifts the burden, for He is strong;
He stills the sigh and awakes the song;
The sorrows that bear me down He shares,
And loves and pardons because He cares.

Let all who are sad take heart again;
We are not alone in our hours of pain;
Our Father looks from His throne above
To soothe and comfort us with His love.
He leaves us not when the storms are high,
And we have safety, for He is nigh;
Can that be trouble which He doth share?
Oh, rest in peace, for the Lord DOES CARE!

Hugh Miller
From *Heart-Warming Poems*. Sword of the Lord Publishers. Used by permission.

CHAPTER 5

The Storms Continue

by Karen Bowman Turner

My mother asked me to write the last chapter of this book. Five months of 1998 were a very trying time for mother and our entire family. From May 12 to the first of August, mother spent approximately one week at home. The remainder was spent in hospitals. Most of those days were spent in intensive care units. It was very stressful for everyone, but the one who suffered most was mother. Through it all, every time we walked into the room, we saw her beautiful smile. Only once when she was fighting for every breath she breathed did I see that smile falter. She told me she was tired and didn't want to fight. The daughter in me refused to accept that, but the nurse in me realized that she was right. I must admit, the daughter won that contest.

On July 6, Mother had a heart catheterization. Afterwards, the doctor told us that the results were not good and as a result complications warranted her being placed back in intensive care. He could not tell us how long she might live, but he recommended that we call the family members in. Later that night the heart surgeon visited with us and told us that her only hope at this point was an experimental procedure called Transverse Myocardial Revascularization (TMR). Using this procedure, the doctor literally burns holes into the heart to allow blood flow. This surgery was only offered at select sites, so the search was on to find a program to accept her. Dallas, Memphis, and numerous other sites turned her down. Finally, the Texas Heart Institute at Saint Luke's Episcopal Hospital in Houston accepted her. She was flown by air ambulance that day.

After being at Saint Luke's for two days we were told that the Federal Drug Administration approval had been withdrawn and they would not be able to do the procedure. The new heart surgeon was willing to try something no one else was willing to do — an almost unheard of fourth coronary artery bypass. The risks were great including bleeding and infection. The doctor was not able to give us hopeful prospects about the outcome. Many people offered prayers to our heavenly Father.

God heard our prayers. After nine hours in surgery the surgeon came out to tell us that he was able to perform four grafts. After three days Mother was moved to a step-down unit. One week later she was discharged to go home.

The recovery period has been slow. My mother does not like to be tied down or slowed down. It is everything she can do to stay within the limitations she has been given.

My mother has always been and continues to be a source of strength to me. When things go wrong in my life, she has always been there for support and she always has a smile.

In my eyes, my mother exemplifies what the wise Solomon said, *"Her children arise up, and call her blessed; her husband also, and he praiseth her. Many daughters have done virtuously, but thou excellest them all. Favour is deceitful, and beauty is vain: but a woman that feareth the* Lord*, she shall be praised. Give her of the fruit of her hands; and let her own works praise her in the gates"* (Proverbs 31:28-31).

Titus also describes a godly woman, *"The aged women likewise, that they be in behaviour as becometh holiness, not false accusers, not given to much wine, teachers of good things; that they may teach the young women to be sober, to love their husbands, to love their children, to be discreet, chaste, keepers at home, good, obedient to their own husbands, that the word of God be not blasphemed"* (Titus 2:3-5).

All of these verses come to mind when I think of my mother. Yes, she has been through many storms in her life. But, yes, she has survived them by keeping her eyes turned to heaven and her faith in Jesus. I am very blessed to have been raised by such a woman. I hope I never forget to thank God daily for her wonderful love and guidance.

Study Guide

This study guide is offered for those who use this book as a group study. Each member of the group should purchase a book. Read the assigned chapter prior to the class when it will be discussed. Give some personal thought to the discussion questions prior to class.

The group should use caution when discussing the storms that have occurred in their lives. Some storms may be too personal to discuss. Details should not be disclosed if they will cause ill feeling or reveal things that would cause another person to have ill feeling toward anyone. Do not insist that class members share details they are not comfortable in sharing or that would hinder another.

Prayerfully consider the discussion of the storms of your lives and those of your church. The common goal of the class members should be to become stronger in the Lord and find comfort in one another. Pray for one another each class session.

Occasionally you will find suggestions to memorize verses of scripture. It is possible for adults to memorize scripture. Take the time to encourage each other and recite the memorized scripture in class — together and individually. A good aid to memorization is to write the verse(s) on index cards and place them in your kitchen, bathroom, and other areas at home where you can read them frequently. You may occasionally find wall hangings that have scripture on them that are comforting during the storms of life. Purchase those and hang them in obvious places in your home. Surround yourself with scripture.